Bygone Bridge of Don

A. Gordon Pirie

Text © A. Gordon Pirie, 2019.
First published in the United Kingdom, 2019,
by Stenlake Publishing Ltd.
Telephone: 01290 551122
www.stenlake.co.uk

Printed by
P2D Books, 1 Newlands Rd,
Westoning, Bedford, MK45 5LD

ISBN 9781840338560

**The publishers regret that they cannot supply
copies of any pictures featured in this book.**

Acknowledgements

The author thanks the following for permission to include their photographs in this book:

Gerald Joss: pages 26, 29, 34, 42, 43, 44.
John Alsop: page 23.
Brian H. Watt: pages 7, 9, 10, 11, 14 (right), 16 (upper), 40, 41, 47 (upper).
George Mauchline: pages 3, 4, 12, 15, 17, 21, 24, 30, 32, 33, 35, 47 (lower).
Grampian Transport Museum: Front cover.
Murcar Links Golf Club: page 48.

Introduction

For much of its history the area now called Bridge of Don was part of the county of Aberdeen and consisted mostly of farms, mansions with their estates, moorland, links and some houses. The road north from Aberdeen ran via Old Aberdeen and crossed the Brig o' Balgownie which was built about 1320. The hamlet immediately to the north of the bridge was known as "Cot Town of Balgownie."

In 1830 a new Bridge of Don was completed which gave a more direct route north via the recently built King Street. A shop, post office and an inn were built alongside the new road. The communities immediately to the north of the new bridge were known as "Damhead" and "Bridge of Don". Over time, the whole area north of the Bridge of Don adopted the name of the bridge leading to it: "Bridge of Don". Attempts were made at times to officially rename the area with its historic title of Balgownie but they came to naught, "Brig' o' Don" already being in common usage.

Aberdeen District Tramways constructed a single track horse-drawn tramline to the end of King Street in 1894. Aberdeen Town Council took over the system to form Aberdeen Corporation Tramways in 1898. Thereafter, the system was electrified and track doubled. At the south end of the bridge at the terminus, various facilities developed both to serve Bridge of Don residents going into town and Aberdeen citizens going for a walk or to play golf.

In the 1930s the area started to expand when Gordon Barracks was built and new houses were built taking advantage of the lower land costs and Aberdeenshire rates. In 1959 the Bridge of Don was widened to create a dual-carriageway. The River Don was the original boundary between the City of Aberdeen and Aberdeenshire, but in 1974 Bridge of Don became part of the city. Over the years, mansions and farm buildings have disappeared and farmland has been built on. Today Bridge of Don is a large suburb in the north of the city of Aberdeen, comprising industrial estates, out-of-town retail outlets as well as shops and housing schemes.

A. Gordon Pirie

The Brig o' Balgownie with a single Gothic arch was built circa 1320 to carry the main road north from Aberdeen. Many modifications and repairs were made over the centuries. The Bridge of Don fund was established in 1605 and accumulated money over the years to pay for repairs and maintenance. The Brig o' Balgownie was the first "Bridge of Don", sometimes thereafter referred to as the "Old Bridge of Don" after the new bridge was erected in 1830. This picture is an aerial view from the 1940s which nicely shows the long approach road to the bridge. The bridge is now closed to vehicular traffic.

The Bridge of Don, Aberdeen.

Between 1827 and 1830 a new bridge was built over the River Don. The old Bridge of Don fund had grown to such an extent that it provided money to pay for the construction of the New Bridge of Don. It was designed by John Smith and Thomas Telford and built of dressed granite. There were five arches, and the parapets had niches for pedestrians to safely stand back from passing traffic. This view is from the 1920s with the Don View Bar at the left. Behind the bar to the right is one of the new houses built in the area, No.2 Don Mouth, which later became No.2 Donmouth Road. Behind it on the horizon is the clubhouse of Royal Aberdeen Golf Club. Further to the right on the horizon is the Coastguard Station surrounded by trees.

A photograph of the new Bridge of Don taken from a point above the old Bridge of Don, the Brig o' Balgownie. Viewing the old bridge from this angle shows the substantial buttresses added to strengthen the structure. The road leads to Cot Town of Balgownie seen on the left. In the foreground is Nether Don Salmon Fishing Station.

William Middleton founded the Balgownie Hall Mission in 1904. He was the superintendent until 1928 when he died at the age of 75. He was originally a ploughboy and had a keen interest in the welfare of farm workers. He had a shop in Belmont Street where he was a patentee and manufacturer. At Balgownie and also on his visits to the country districts, he was often accompanied by evangelist Hatashi-Masha-Katish (one of many spellings). He was a Sudanese prince who had been rescued from slavery by General Gordon. The photograph shows William Middleton and his Balgownie Bell Boys standing in front of the Brig o' Balgownie. His hand-bell ringers performed at religious meetings and entertained Bridge of Don residents at functions, including greeting people on arrival at their new homes by playing a selection of tunes. A granite stone built into the gable end of the mission hall commemorates his life and work.

The Aberdeen Golf Club was originally founded in 1780 as the Society of Golfers at Aberdeen. From 1815 the members played on Queen's Links but then moved to a new home on Balgownie Links in 1888. The original Balgownie clubhouse is seen above. The club became The Royal Aberdeen Golf Club in 1903. To the right is the clubhouse for Aberdeen Ladies Golf Club founded in 1892.

Perwinnes Moss or Scotstown Moor (also with the spelling of Scotstoun or Scotston) was originally part of the Bishopric of Aberdeen during medieval times. It was a commonty, an area of land where people were entitled to obtain fuel and graze their animals. Scotstown Moor Camp for Ailing Children was set up in 1905 to provide annual summer holidays for deprived children in Aberdeen who were in need of fresh air, wholesome food and exercise. It was a charitable organisation funded locally by donations, subscriptions and fund-raising events. The photograph above is from one of the first years in operation when 100-150 children were provided for under canvas.

The photograph above can be dated to summer 1907 showing the building constructed earlier in that year which housed a kitchen, bathroom and a bedroom for the female staff. On Sundays, families and other visitors came to the camp for religious services, sports and entertainments. Crowds of over 3,000 were often recorded. In later years it was referred to as The Scotstown Moor Children's Camp.

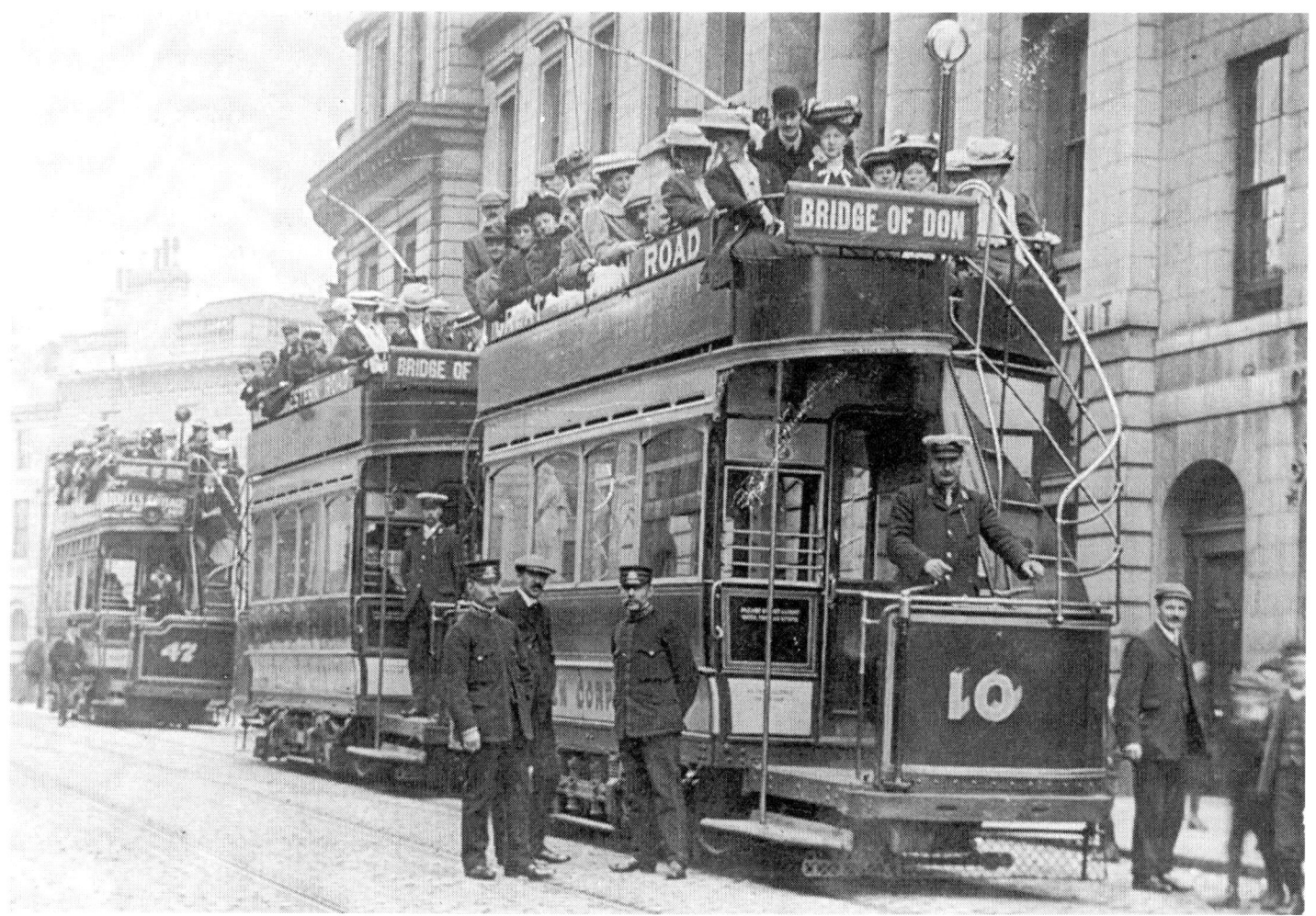

Bridge of Don was a popular destination for the citizens of Aberdeen, going for walks, picnics or attending special events. In the photograph above three open-top trams with Bridge of Don headboards are sitting at the corner of King Street and Castle Street. Two inspectors are supervising the loading and departure. It would appear that most, if not all the travellers have decided to sit on the top deck to enjoy the view. The tram numbers and designs indicate sometime between about 1905 to 1910 therefore it is quite probable that this depicted one of the first special trips for the Sunday entertainments at Scotstown. Other forms of transport were laid on to convey the people from the tram terminus.

The above scene from a Sunday in the early 1920s shows crowds at Scotstown Moor Children's Camp being entertained by the band of the 4th Battalion Gordon Highlanders. The photograph was taken by James C. Esslemont, official photographer to the Gordon Highlanders who lived at Brighouse, Brig o' Balgownie. By the 1930s permanent dormitories had been built. With this improved accommodation, up to 600 children were being catered for during the holiday season. During the war a radio direction finding station was established and after 1940 the children's camp had to close. Attempts were made to continue but the camp was wound up in 1952. After the war, because of a shortage of housing, a shanty town of over 40 dwellings developed on Scotstown Moor and on plots let by the Scotstown Estate. Shacks, huts, converted railway carriages and old buses provided homes. The buildings were demolished in 1954. In 1972 the area was designated as a Site of Special Scientific Interest (SSSI). Since 1994 it has been managed as a Local Nature Reserve.

In this view circa 1910 Don Mills is at the extreme left. This was originally built as a distillery in 1794 with a 400ft long quay enabling boats to load and unload cargo alongside. The venture was unsuccessful, however, and the property was advertised for sale from 1796. From 1805 at least the premises were in use as a mill. Meal, flour and barley were produced throughout the 19th century. Water and steam powered the machinery. Water to the mill was originally supplied from a dam higher up the slope to the east of Ellon Road. The water powered an upper wheel which in turn turned a second wheel below. During the Second World War as "Ogston's Mills", meal and cattle feed was being produced 24 hours a day by a workforce of twenty. The mill continued throughout the 1950s but then closed. The quay and water culvert are still clearly visible.

The postcard on the left shows a rather serene scene with an Edwardian lady sitting on an upturned boat on the banks of the Don, near the Brig o' Balgownie. The postcard on the right commemorates a young woman of a more intrepid nature for the period who reached the banks of the River Don by other means. Topsy Johnson was a singer, actress and comedienne. She was also a keen swimmer and the first female to successfully swim from the River Dee to the River Don. This feat was accomplished on a Monday evening in September 1908 after she had given a performance at the Beach Pavilion the same day. She was aged 19 at the time.

Salmon fishers seen working at the mouth of the River Don in the early 1900s. Salmon had formerly comprised a major part of the diet of the citizens and Aberdeen had long been a major exporter of salmon. The fishing rights had been granted by the Crown through the centuries. The fish were caught either by using stake nets or bag nets. The Bridge of Don is in the background and at the right hand side can be seen the cottages of the Coastguard station.

Salmon fishing taking place at the Cruives of Don. Cruives were man-made weirs designed to trap salmon. Both views are from postcards, the top one with a halfpenny stamp in 1914 and the bottom one with a penny stamp in 1918. It is obvious that the two photographs were taken at the same time though, perhaps around 1910. Salmon fishers used a flat-bottom rowing boat called a coble which can be seen in the bottom scene.

The photograph shows Balgownie House circa 1910-1920, previously the seat of the Lairds of Balgownie for many centuries. From the earliest mention in the early 1300s the spelling changed over the years; Polgouny, Polgowny or Polgownie. The name also changed when under new ownership. In the late 1600s the estate was renamed Cairnfield by the Gray family and in 1721 when William Fraser, son of Lord Saltoun bought the estate of Balgownie he renamed it Fraserfield. Margaret Fraser of Fraserfield inherited the properties in 1817 and married Henry David Forbes. During their period of ownership the name Balgownie was restored. After the last member of the family died in 1893 the estate was managed by trustees. At times the mansion was unoccupied. It was used as a nursing home from 1922 until 1935 when it was sold and again used as a private home. The building was demolished in 1969.

This view of Ellon Road dates from about 1910. The photograph was taken from a point at the north end of the Bridge of Don looking north. On the right is the original Don View Hotel. Up the slope are two granite buildings and the junction with Links Road is heading off to the right. It would appear to be a special occasion, judging from the crowd of people dressed in their Sunday best, most walking north after alighting from a tram. A likely destination would be Scotstown Children's Camp.

The junction of what is now Balgownie Road and Scotstown Road showing Braehead Croft on the right and the Bridge of Don School which was opened in 1895. This view appears to be from the early 1900s. During the Second World War it was a First Aid Post for the area. It was used for infants after Bridge of Don Academy on North Donside Road was opened in 1943 and also housed a canteen providing food for both schools. Between 1964 and 1973 St. Nicholas School used the building. It was later as a nursery school and now houses St. Nicholas Pupil Support Centre.

The view above shows Balgownie Lodge around 1910-1920. Polgownie Lodge as it was originally known was designed by John Smith (Tudor Johnnie) in the 1820s. It was the residence of the Crombie family of Grandholm from the second half of the 19th century until the 1930s. In 1947 the Scottish Episcopal Church converted the building and it was in use as an eventide home until 1967. The University of Aberdeen then made use of it as student halls of residence. It was listed in 1981, restored in 1986 to be integrated into Aberdeen Science and Technology Park and is now part of the Balgownie Centre, Campus 3, Aberdeen Innovation Park.

Gardeners working at Balgownie Lodge in the early 1900s.

As its name suggests The Seaton Brick and Tile Company Limited originated in Seaton. As supplies of clay were used up the company moved to Torry, then in 1898 the company built a new brickworks at Strabathie (Blackdog). This photograph of 1905 shows how the clay was dug by squads of four men, then put in tubs which were hauled by an endless chain up a conveyor to be processed and made into bricks and tiles. The company built the three foot gauge Strabathie Light Railway to carry its products to a terminus at Bridge of Don. The company ceased operations in 1924.

A Seaton Brick & Tile Co. train is seen here about 1905. The locomotive was built by Hudswell Clarke of Leeds and was named "NEWBURGH". The carriages had been converted from horse-drawn tramcars formerly used on the Woodside route and were used to transport the workers between Bridge of Don and Strabathie brickworks. This train is heading south towards Bridge of Don along Murcar Links past Blackdog Rock which can just be seen as a dark triangle at the centre right of the photograph. The landscape has changed since then because sand has built up over the years so Blackdog Rock is no longer visible from this viewpoint because of the intervening dunes.

The terminus of the Strabathie Light Railway was located on Links Road, Bridge of Don. As the name suggests, the Seaton Brick & Tile Co. Ltd manufactured bricks and tiles. Most of the tiles were agricultural drainage tiles. Originally these were two-piece items with a flat tile at the bottom but by this period one-piece pipes were being produced. They were still referred to as drainage tiles though. In the photograph above from circa 1910 tens of thousands of these pipes are stacked along Links Road ready for purchase by landowners and farmers. Traditionally field drainage ditches were dug after the harvest and throughout the winter period. Behind the pipes is the mill dam and its sluice gate which supplied Don Mills. The dam later became the site of D.C. Stewart, building contractor. Ellon Road runs from left to right, the area behind the dam being known as Damhead. The granite buildings visible at the left are now Nos. 20 to 30 Ellon Road.

The Coastguard was formed as a development of former organisations whose primary function was to prevent smuggling. Over the years during the 1800s, assisting ships in distress and saving lives gained precedence. This early 1900s view of the Bridge of Don Coastguard station shows the housing provided for the staff which was typical in having a two-storey home for the Chief Officer with adjoining terraced cottages for the other personnel. Traditionally a shared corridor ran inside the length of the cottages so that men could be roused quickly in the event of an emergency. They faced south onto the River Don with vegetable gardens at the front. The most notable resident was Thomas Blake Glover, the "Scottish Samurai". The Glover family lived there from 1849 to 1864 when his father Lieutenant Thomas Berry Glover was commander of the station. The roofs were originally thatched, being replaced later by corrugated iron. More up to date housing was constructed alongside in the 1920s, but these old cottages still stood for decades thereafter before being demolished.

To reinforce the men of the Coastguard the Board of Trade encouraged the formation of volunteer life-saving brigades. Life-saving equipment was issued to the volunteers who were to be trained by the Chief Officer of HM Coastguard. The rocket-propelled life-saving apparatus was fitted to a cart and housed in a special shed. The cart would be drawn down to the shoreline, rockets with rescue lines attached would be fired at the vessel in distress and the survivors hauled ashore by breeches buoy. Volunteer members of the Bridge of Don LSA (Life Saving Apparatus) crew are seen training on a Saturday afternoon in the 1950s. From left to right are Messrs: Booth, Baxter, Tawse, Sim, McLean (wearing the lifejacket), Douglas (of HM Coastguard) and McEwan.

Denmore House was originally built as a hunting lodge for the 4th Duke of Gordon in 1790. The estate was later purchased by George Charles Moir who extended the property in the 19th century. Thomas Adam (1842-1919) an Aberdeen ship-owner bought the Denmore Estate and took over the residence in 1900. The view above is from the period 1910-1920. His son Thomas Livingston Adam (1880-1959) had the house re-modelled in 1920. Upon his death, the estate passed to his son Major Thomas Adam (1914-1985).

This view shows the rear of Denmore House from the same period, 1910-1920. In 1972 Major Tom Adam sold Denmore House and grounds to Salvesen Homes Ltd., with the understanding that the building would be preserved. In February 1974 the company was given permission for a development of 250 houses which would involve demolition. Major Adam, joined by the Aberdeen branch of the Georgian Society, wrote to the Scottish Secretary of State requesting that the building be listed. Aberdeen County Council issued a preservation notice in June. A government inspector visited the site in September 1974 with a view to advising the Scottish Secretary on whether the building should be listed as being of historical interest. Salvesen Homes stated that they would investigate the possibility of preserving the house but gave no commitment. It was suggested that the house could be retained as clubhouse for the residents, but it was decided the cost of upkeep would be too high. The building fell into disrepair and was demolished in 1979. The loch and some of the grounds have been retained as residential amenities on the new housing scheme called Denmore Park.

John Joss, the chauffeur at Denmore House is seen here in a car of French manufacture sometime after 1910. Mrs. Eliza Joss is standing at the doorway in the background and Ben the dog is sitting in front of the vehicle. After his sons had returned from the Great War, he went on to found John Joss & Sons, a lorry haulage company. The Adam family of Denmore helped to set up the business on condition that Jim, one of the sons, remained in service as a chauffeur.

Scotstown House was built by Archibald Simpson in 1824 for the Moirs of Scotstown and Spital. Rounded bows of the Regency style and Ionic columns at the front express the social status of a family of substance. The estate included stables, coach-house, gate-houses and an underground ice-house all set amongst lawns and trees with a lake, encircled by a rubble wall. The above photographs show Scotstown House as it appeared about 1910-20. The mansion barely lasted for a century though. After William Bean Moir died, the house and estate was purchased in 1922 by Alexander Black Reid. He was an Aberdeen timber merchant who owned Scotstown Sawmills. He did not live in Scotstown House which was left vacant and officially described as uninhabitable two years later. The mansion was left derelict and fell into a ruinous condition for well over three decades and was subsequently demolished. The boundary wall can still be seen along Scotstown Road, behind which are the remains of the estate trees and shrubs including rhododendron bushes.

The tramway terminus at the Bridge of Don looking north circa 1910. The postcard postmarked 1913 is entitled "Sunday night at the Bridge of Don, a rush for the last car" The tram, No.45, was built in 1903 as an open-topped electric vehicle, being fitted with a top cover in 1907. The route was double track all the way up King Street to the terminus at the Bridge of Don. Here you can see the points to allow the tram to move forward and then return on the left hand side track again to the Bridge of Dee.

THE POST OFFICE, BRIDGE OF DON, ABERDEEN.

The Bridge of Don Post Office is depicted above on a postcard specially printed for James Thomson, Post Office, Bridge of Don. It was situated on the corner of Balgownie Road and Ellon Road, the front door of the house faced onto Ellon Road. The post office had previously been run from Greig's premises at the shop on the corner of Ellon Road and Links Road. The building seen above was constructed in the summer of 1914 for James Thomson's home and business of stationer and tobacconist. He had been appointed to the position of sub-postmaster and served from these new premises. However, he died in November 1917 so this post office was short-lived. Henry John Watson was appointed as his replacement in January 1918. He had acquired the former Greig business and so the post office returned to its former location. This building above known variously as Holmlea, Homelea or Holm Lea, under various owners, served as business premises and eventually purely as a house by which time the gable end window and shop door had been blocked up. In 1920 the war memorial was erected to the left of the property. The building was demolished as part of the traffic improvement scheme which involved the widening of the Bridge of Don, Ellon Road and the junction with Balgownie Road between 1957 and 1959. The war memorial was then moved to where the building had previously been.

A large group of men are seen posing at the Brig o' Balgownie in late 1914 after war had been declared. Some are in full uniform, the cap badge and lanyards indicating Royal Artillery. At the time there were two territorial units based in Aberdeen. No. 1 Company, North Scottish Royal Garrison Artillery was based at the barracks in Fonthill Road and 1st Highland Brigade, Royal Field Artillery was in North Silver Street. The men were not obliged to serve overseas but the vast majority did volunteer. From September 1914 a recruiting drive took place to double the manpower so that a reserve could be formed. We can surmise that the men in civilian clothing are new volunteers and probably Royal Field Artillery. There was a severe shortage of uniforms due to the overwhelming response to the call for volunteers all over Britain. They do appear to be rather well dressed though, in their Sunday best with collar and tie. Perhaps the photograph was taken after church parade or simply they had all been reminded to get spruced up for the special occasion. Many have adopted the customary photographic pose for soldiers at that time: "nonchalant expression, with unlit fag dangling from the mouth". The building behind was "Brig End", now 259/261 Don Street.

This photograph was taken in the 1920s in front of the shop at the corner of Links Road and Ellon Road. The lorry is a Thornycroft J-Type introduced in 1913 and manufactured in thousands during the Great War. After the war many army surplus vehicles were purchased for civilian use, bought by former soldiers who had been taught to drive during the war. Standing in front of the lorry are the Joss brothers, from left to right: Willie, Jack and Bert. At the left of the picture opposite the shop is the granite house "Holmlea" which was later demolished between 1957 and 1959 during road widening.

Donbank Tea Rooms were located at 15 Balgownie Road. Mr. and Mrs. Smith were the proprietors from 1918 until 1943. At the time when it was most popular, the premises had an uninterrupted view down the slope to the River Don and the North Sea. In addition to being frequented by walkers they were also used a local meeting place for whist drives and political meetings. The gable end of the building was whitewashed and had large black letters spelling TEAS. The faded remains can be seen to this day.

A 1931 aerial view of the Bridge of Don and the island known as "Allochy" looking east. To the left we see The Don Bar and Don Mills. Balgownie Road winds left and right at the bottom of the photograph. To the right is the tramway terminus and shop and the wide Beach Esplanade. The area was still quite open; trees have since grown up on the banks and houses have been built between Balgownie Road and the river.

A view of Bridge of Don in the 1930s. The war memorial was unveiled in 1920 and the gas lamp fitted on top provided the only street lighting for many years. The smaller building with its gable end facing the street was specially built for the post office. A shop is sited at the corner of Ellon Road and Links Road. The shop proprietor had always traditionally been the sub-postmaster. William Grieg ran the shop during the 1800s, son George taking over at the turn of the century. At this time the corner shop was run by Alexander Scott Law (Scottie Law), then from 1933 by George Law (no relation). The lorry is sitting on top of the public weighbridge. On the right of the photograph the garage at the rear of the shop housed a horse-drawn cart for delivering groceries around the area but was destroyed by a German bomb in 1943. The corner building was taken over by The Clydesdale Bank in 1974 to become the first bank in Bridge of Don. The bank is now closed and a funeral director occupies the premises.

This photograph was taken in the early 1930s from the south side of the River Don. To the left at the south of the bridge are the tramway terminus, houses, shops, tearoom, toilets and putting green. On the right behind the buildings is open farmland. Further, on the far horizon is more farmland and trees forming part of Denmore House estate and Scotstown House estates.

In 1932 construction started on Gordon Barracks. It was opened in 1935 providing a new home for the Gordon Highlanders who had previously been based at Castlehill Barracks. The top photograph showing the new barracks was taken from a point opposite which was still an open field. Ellon Road runs from left to right in the middle of the picture past the main gate but is obscured by the long grass. The building at the extreme left is sited at the corner of Ellon Road and Hutcheon Gardens. This was the police house and police station of Aberdeenshire Constabulary which was built during the same period. The building is now in use as a veterinary practice. In the bottom photograph, the figure just visible behind the railings is the postie with his bike. In 1964 Gordon Barracks became the HQ of the Highland Brigade. Then, as the Scottish Infantry Depot, it was used as a recruit training camp until 1986. The Territorial Army moved in during 1985. It is now known as Gordon Barracks Reserve and Cadet Centre.

A formal opening ceremony was held on Saturday 14th September 1935. In the morning, Lord Provost Henry Alexander took the salute from the Town House on the Gordons' departure from Castlehill Depot. In the afternoon Gordon Highlanders, ex-servicemen and the pipe band gathered on the promenade. General Sir Ian Hamilton then led them over the Bridge of Don and into their new home. The Marquis of Huntly, Chief of Clan Gordon and General Sir Ian Hamilton, Colonel-in-Chief are seen above inspecting the troops in the new barracks square.

A post-war aerial view of Gordon Barracks. There are a great many Nissen huts interspersed between the original granite buildings. To the north side, at the left of the photograph, are extra wooden barrack blocks built to cater for wartime personnel. At the bottom left Ellon Road is a dual carriageway, completed in the late 1930s and provided with footpaths and cycle tracks on both sides.

On Armistice Day, 11th November 1947, a procession marches along Links Road led by George Law. Heading the main body is Piper George Clark followed by members of the British Legion including John (Jack) Joss, George Maitland and Postie John Taylor. Behind them are representatives of youth organisations including the Boys Brigade, Boy Scouts and Girl Guides.

Jack Joss is seen laying a wreath at the memorial while Piper Clark is at the right of the picture. The war memorial with attached horse trough dedicated to the fallen of the parish of Oldmachar (north of the Don) was unveiled on the 1st May 1920. It stood in the middle of Balgownie Road and had to be moved to its present location as part of the Bridge of Don and Ellon Road widening scheme between 1956 and 1958.

After the Seaton Brick & Tile Co. ceased operations in 1924 the depot was taken over by John Joss & Sons, haulage contractors. The supply of sand gradually became the main business. In the early 1950s the company employed over 50 men. A photograph above from that time shows the yard on Links Road with the granite house "Tilquhillie" on the right. Standing in front of the John Joss & Sons lorry are from left to right: Eddie Grant and Frankie McRobb. In 2000 the company was sold but still operates under the Joss name from Lochhills Quarry, Parkhill. Flats have been built on the site, which has been named Joss Court.

The tramway terminus and shelter at the Bridge of Don looking north in 1953. To the left is Pirie's shop. Just over the bridge is the Don View Bar. This photograph shows No. 20, one of the 76-seater bogie streamliner trams introduced in 1949 which were used on the "Bridges Route" between the Bridge of Don and the Bridge of Dee. Before conversion to automatic door operation, they had a three man crew; one driver and two conductors. Looking behind the tram we can see how narrow the Bridge of Don was with vehicles, cyclists and pedestrians all vying for space.

This photograph was taken on 3rd May 1958, the last day of operation for trams running to the Bridge of Don. No.103, a Peckham tram of 1925 vintage rests on the left. Alongside is a Metro Cammell "Orion" bodied AEC Regent V255 one of the new double-decker replacement buses. A few weeks later, all of Aberdeen's trams were unceremoniously burnt for scrap on Queen's Links. Behind the tram fencing has been erected at the Bridge of Don which was being widened at the time.

The Bridge of Don was widened to form a dual-carriageway between 1957 and 1959. This was achieved by building a duplicate bridge built of concrete to the same design alongside it on the east and then using new granite for facing and reinstating the original parapets. The new road surface was tarmac. Shops and houses at both ends of the bridge were demolished and the bungalows on Ellon Road lost most of their front gardens. The lower photograph was taken looking south from the site of the original Don View Bar which was demolished and replaced by a new bar. The bridge was officially opened by the Queen Mother on Monday 25th May 1959. The top view is looking north showing the new pub. Daylight can be seen between the arches reminding us that the bridge is in effect two bridges side by side.

This photograph was taken in 1961 at the Northern Open at Murcar Golf Club. In the background is the Hill of Strabathie, formerly known as Tarbathy Hill or Tarbathie Hill, a prominent landmark familiar to locals and homecoming sailors. On the summit was what was often called "Strabathie Castle", an oval building with a conical roof thatched with heather. It was thought that the building was originally constructed to house the theodolite used by the Ordnance Survey. A triangulation point on the hill was one end of a primary baseline during the 1817 trigonometric survey of Great Britain. The building was later utilised as a shooting lodge and a private bathing station by Parkhill lairds and families. The hill originally stood at 170 ft above sea level but excavations and levelling off over the years have greatly reduced its height. More recently it has been used as a landfill site.